GOD SAID IT

OLD TESTAMENT HEROES—2

BRADLEY BOOTH

Pacific Press®
Publishing Association
Nampa, Idaho | www.pacificpress.com

Cover design by Gerald Lee Monks
Cover design resources from Marcus Mashburn
Inside design by Gerald Lee Monks
Inside illustrations by Marcus Mashburn

The author assumes full responsibility for the accuracy of all facts and
quotations as cited in this book.

All Scripture quotations are from the New King James Version®. Copyright ©
1982 by Thomas Nelson. Used by permission. All rights reserved.

You can obtain additional copies of this book by calling toll-free 1-800-765-6955
or by visiting AdventistBookCenter.com.

978-0-8163-6538-8

November 2019

CONTENTS

COLORING PAGES

Check out the coloring pages in the middle of this book. They are based on the featured stories and are meant to be colored in by the reader and presented as a gift to a person they appreciate. These may include

- parents,
- sisters or brothers,
- grandparents,
- aunts and uncles,
- teachers,
- neighbors, or
- friends.

INTRODUCTION

God Said It introduces children to the Bible. It is designed to help children understand the importance of reading and learning from the Word of God. Our prayer is that parents, teachers, church visitors, and children everywhere will use this book to reach young people for Jesus.

The Bible is full of stories about heroes who were faithful as they led God's people and the results of what happened when they sometimes were not. In this book you'll read a story about a boy named Samuel, who talked with God. You'll read about Saul, a farmer, who became the first king of Israel. There are also two exciting stories about David the shepherd boy, who fought lions, and David the warrior, who fought the giant Goliath.

God Said It is dedicated to God's faithful witnesses in the Bible and to all the boys and girls who read these stories. We trust that the stories on these pages will draw children to Jesus. May they choose to be faithful like the Bible heroes from long ago so that they can one day shine "like the stars forever" (Daniel 12:3, NKJV).

SAMUEL:
THE BOY WHO LISTENED
THIS STORY IS FOUND IN 1 SAMUEL 1-3

amuel was an answer to prayer. His mother, Hannah, had wanted a baby boy for many years, but for some reason, the baby never came. And then one day, she prayed that if God gave her a baby boy, she would dedicate him to serve God at the tabernacle sanctuary.

God heard her prayer. One day she finally had that baby and was so happy about it. When he was old enough to leave home, she took him to the sanctuary to live with Priest Eli. Then every year she would visit and bring him a new robe to wear.

Samuel was a little boy, but he could do all kinds of things to help Priest Eli in the tabernacle sanctuary. Ashes had to be emptied from the altar for burnt offerings. Water was needed for the priests to wash every day. Oil must be put in the seven-branched candlesticks, and the wicks had to be trimmed.

It was wonderful for Eli to have someone around he could depend on. His own two sons, Hophni and Phineas, were not much help. They were spoiled in many ways and troublemakers of the worst sort. They didn't seem to care about anything except having parties, getting drunk, and stealing from the worshipers at the sanctuary. A prophet of God came by to tell Eli he must make his boys stop doing bad things or they would be punished, but Eli did not make them behave.

These were the kinds of things going on at the sanctuary when Samuel came to live with Eli. The old priest must have often wished his sons were more like young Samuel.

One evening, Samuel went to bed as usual. After saying his prayers, he lay down on his little mat to sleep, and just as he was dozing off, he heard a Voice calling him.

"Samuel! Samuel!" the Voice said.

Samuel thought Priest Eli was calling him, so he jumped up and ran to where the old man was sleeping. "I'm here," Samuel said in the darkness. "What do you need?"

Eli shook his head. "I didn't call you, son. Go lie down."

Samuel was surprised, but he went back to his bed as he was told.

Three times the Voice called him, and three times Samuel ran to Eli to find out what the old priest needed.

By now Eli knew it must be God who was trying to talk with Samuel. "Go and lie down," he told the boy, "and if the Voice calls you again, just say, 'Speak, Lord, for your servant is listening.'"

So Samuel went and lay down on his bed, and sure enough, the Voice came again. "Samuel! Samuel!"

Samuel must have been excited and a little bit frightened to hear God speaking to him. He tried to remember what he was supposed to say, but all he could think of was, "Speak, for your servant is listening."

And God did speak to Samuel. He told him all that was going to happen to Eli's family. It was a very serious message for the Lord to give a little boy, but no one else at the sanctuary was listening for God's voice. "Trouble is coming to Priest Eli and his sons, and it cannot be stopped!" God said. "Because his sons have been so evil, they are both going to die on the same day!"

The next morning Eli wanted to know what God had said to Samuel the night before. We can imagine the little boy bowing his head in sadness as he told Eli the terrible message, but the old priest humbly accepted it.

"The Lord is good," Eli said. "Let Him do what He thinks is best."

Having to give Priest Eli such a message must have been a hard thing for little Samuel to do, but he obeyed God and did it bravely. This was the beginning of many great things Samuel would do for God as he grew up, and it all began that night when he was a little boy.

SAUL:
ISRAEL'S FIRST KING
THIS STORY IS FOUND IN 1 SAMUEL 9–31

When God's people came into the land of Canaan from Egypt, they did not have a king. In those days, kings ruled over countries or sometimes just one city, but God did not want His people to have that kind of government. He wanted the people to rule themselves with the help of prophets, priests, and judges, and that's the way it was for several hundred years.

Unfortunately, the people finally decided they wanted a king like all the nations around them, so Saul, from the tribe of Benjamin, was chosen to be their first king. For a few years, things went well. God was with King Saul as he led the Israelite army into battle against the Ammonites and helped them win a great victory. Everyone was so thankful to God. However, King Saul soon became proud of his accomplishments as king.

In an important battle, he defeated a dangerous enemy and then brought back cattle and sheep as trophies of the war. The prophet Samuel had told King Saul not to do this, but the king did it anyway.

Another time before going into battle, King Saul decided to offer a sacrifice in order to get God's blessing. This was something only the priests were supposed to do, but the king did it.

"Because you keep disobeying God, He will take the kingdom away from you," the prophet Samuel said. King Saul didn't like it and got angry, but after that, Samuel didn't come to see him anymore.

When David fought and killed Goliath, the Philistine

giant, King Saul asked David to be his personal body-guard. David was a brave warrior, and he played the harp well.

Soon David was the most popular man in Israel. He became best friends with Jonathan, the king's son, and King Saul even gave the princess Michal to David to be his wife.

SAMUEL:
THE BOY WHO LISTENED
1 SAMUEL 1-3

This is a gift for _____.

From _____

SAUL:
ISRAEL'S FIRST KING
1 SAMUEL 9-31

This is a gift for _____.

From _____

DAVID:
THE SHEPHERD BOY
1 SAMUEL 16 AND 17

This is a gift for _____.

From _____

DAVID
AND GOLIATH
1 SAMUEL 17

This is a gift for _____.

From _____

Not surprisingly, the king soon became jealous of David. One day, while David was playing his harp for the king in the throne room, King Saul threw a javelin at David, trying to kill him. But David escaped and fled for his life, so Saul chased him with his army. When the king discovered some priests had given David food for his journey, he got very angry and killed the whole family of priests.

By now the nation knew king Saul was acting like a madman, but no one could stop him. He was the king, and in those days, kings had too much power.

For several years King Saul hunted David. The young man and his warrior friends fled from place to place, hiding in the mountain caves of the desert, and always the king was not far behind. Several times the king almost caught David. A couple of times David could have killed King Saul, but he always spared the king's life.

When the Philistines came to battle the Israelite armies once again, King Saul was afraid. He had killed the priests, the prophet Samuel was dead, and David was on the run, so now the king had no one to turn to for advice from God.

Finally, he went to a witch who lived in a cave and asked her how the battle with the Philistines would turn out. She worked with Satan to bring up a demon in the form of a ghost. The demon told King Saul that he and his three sons would die tragically in battle the next day, and that's exactly what happened because God was no longer protecting the king.

It was a very hard lesson for everyone in Israel to learn. Having a king rule over them was a bad idea because if the king was not a good man, the nation would suffer.

The Bible is full of stories like this one. If we will obey God and keep His commandments, He will bless us in so many ways. If we do not, things may turn out for us as they did for King Saul.

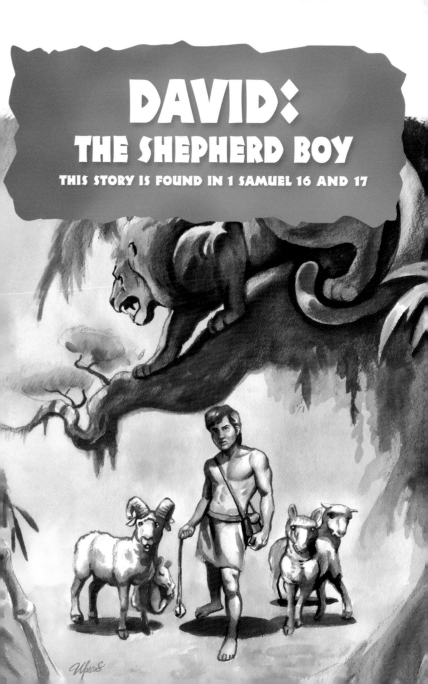

DAVID:
THE SHEPHERD BOY
THIS STORY IS FOUND IN 1 SAMUEL 16 AND 17

avid grew up in the village of Bethlehem, where most people worked on farms and raised animals for a living. He came from a big family, so there was always lots to do.

As the youngest of eight brothers, David's job was to take care of his father's flock of sheep. In the morning he took them out to graze on the grassy hills surrounding Bethlehem. At least twice daily, he made sure they had enough water to drink. At night he locked them up in a sheepfold or stayed with them out in the fields when he was far away from home. Sometimes his cousins, Joab and Abishai, would come out to help him guard the sheep, but often David was by himself.

It could be scary out in the wilderness, and guarding sheep as a shepherd was no easy task for a boy. He had to be constantly on the lookout for bandits or wild animals that might hunt the sheep.

David didn't have much choice about being a shepherd, but for the most part, he liked the job. Being out on the grassy hills was more fun than plowing fields or harvesting crops. And he always felt closer to God when he was by himself in the wide-open spaces.

He loved to sing about the God of heaven and often played songs on a lyre, an instrument something like a harp. He would play his lyre while the sheep were resting in the shade at noonday or around the campfire at night when they were sleeping. That was when he wrote many of the psalms we find in our Bible today.

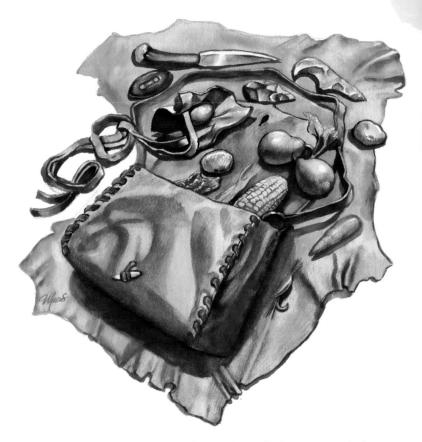

    While guarding the sheep, David always carried a
stick called a shepherd's staff. He used it to guide the
sheep where they needed to go or protect them from
poisonous snakes and scorpions. He also carried a
leather pouch at his side to store food, a piece of flint
for starting a campfire, and stones to use in his sling.

    Of all the tools David might need as a shepherd,
the sling proved to be the most helpful. He practiced
with it day and night until he could hit any target with

great accuracy. With this weapon, he could scare off thieves or bandits who might want to steal from his flock. And of course, wild animals were a constant threat to the sheep.

At times like this, David's sling was a deadly weapon. He used it to chase off wild predators and

even killed some of them in order to protect his sheep. Packs of wolves prowled the hills of Bethlehem in the days of David, and sometimes he had to fight them with his sling. Bears lived in the mountain forests and were also enemies of the sheep. But it was the lions David feared most. They would sometimes hunt the sheep even in broad daylight to capture a ewe or stray lamb.

If a lion jumped from a rock or cliff and landed in the middle of his flock to scatter the sheep, David had to be ready. In a flash the beast could grab a helpless lamb and turn to make its escape, but David was brave. It was no time for a boy to be afraid if he wanted to save his flock. Quick as a wink, his hand would go into his shepherd's pouch for a smooth, round stone. Into the sling it would go, and then he would whirl the sling around and around his head. Straight in the direction of the escaping lion the stone would fly, hitting it and bringing it down.

In this way David rescued his sheep and saved the lives of many little lambs. There was nothing he wouldn't do to protect his father's flock of sheep, but he always knew it was God who gave him the courage to do it.

DAVID
AND GOLIATH
THIS STORY IS FOUND IN 1 SAMUEL 17

**W**hat kinds of things are kids afraid of? Needles? Spiders? The dark? How about giants? That's what this story is about— the most famous giant in history. Everybody was afraid of him. The Bible tells us his name was Goliath and that he was nine and a half feet tall. That's really tall!

He lived a long time ago, but you've probably heard of him. He was a Philistine giant and had come to fight the Israelites. For forty days, he had been marching out to the battlefield to make fun of King Saul and his army. Even worse, he was making fun of God.

King Saul was afraid of Goliath just like everybody else, but what could he do? The giant was too huge and fierce for any of them to fight.

And then David the shepherd boy showed up. He had come to bring his older brothers some food from home, and when he heard Goliath mocking God and taunting the Israelite soldiers, he was very upset.

"Why do you allow this big, bad giant to curse God?" he demanded. "It's not right! If no one will go fight him, I will!"

King Saul heard about the shepherd boy in his camp who was not afraid to stand up against a giant. He sent for David but told him he was too young to fight the massive Philistine soldier.

David disagreed. "I've killed lions and bears while guarding my father's sheep," he told the king, "and I will kill this giant."

The king was surprised at David's bravery and finally agreed to let him fight. He gave David his own sword and armor, but David wouldn't wear them. Instead, he marched out to the battlefield with only a shepherd's rod, his sling, and a leather shepherd's pouch.

When Goliath saw him coming, he was very angry. "Am I a dog that you would come out to fight me with a stick?" he roared (see 1 Samuel 17:43). "Come over here, boy! When I'm done with you, the vultures and jackals will have you for supper!"

David crossed the small stream running through the valley and picked up five smooth stones as he headed for the giant. He might have been afraid, but he didn't show it.

"You come to me with a sword, a spear, and a javelin," David bravely shouted, "but I come to you in the name of the LORD of hosts. He is the God of the armies of Israel whom you have cursed, but He doesn't need swords and spears to win a battle. Today He is going to help me beat you so that the whole world will know there is a God in heaven" (see 1 Samuel 17:45, 46).

When Goliath heard David's words, his face went red with rage. He swung his sword wildly from side to side as he strode toward David, but the shepherd boy was ready.

Into David's sling went a smooth stone from the riverbed, and round and round he swung it over his head as he ran toward the giant. Zing! The stone flew from the sling straight at the giant's forehead, and down Goliath fell like a big tree.

David grabbed Goliath's heavy sword and, quick as a wink, finished the giant by cutting off his head. The battle was over before it even had a chance to start.

The Israelite soldiers cheered and then chased the frightened Philistine soldiers all the way back to

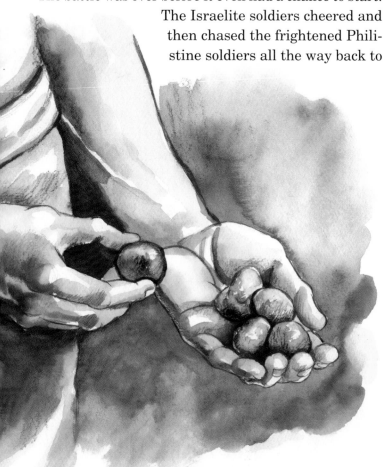

their country. It was a big victory for the Israelite army and for David the shepherd boy. God had rescued His people from the Philistines because a boy was brave enough to call on Him for help.

God still wants us to ask Him for help when we face giants, even if they aren't real ones like Goliath. He wants us to call on Him when things are looking good too. He will always come to our rescue when we trust in Him, just as He did for David the shepherd boy so long ago.

Want to know more
to know more
about what
God said?

It's easy with FREE eBooklets & Bible Guides just for you!

1 Go to **kidsvop.com**
2 Click on Bible Guides
3 Get started!

To receive KidZone in print, go to
KidsBibleinfo.com/request

Your parents
can also learn more
about what God says
at **Bibleinfo.com**

voice of prophecy